Stone Upon Stone

Stone Upon Stone
Psalms of Remembrance

Selected Poetry of Lonnell E. Johnson

Jubilee! PRESS™
an imprint of Imagine! Books™ • Columbus Ohio

Stone Upon Stone: Psalms of Remembrance
First Edition

Copyright © 2005 by Lonnell E. Johnson

All rights reserved. No part of this publication may be reproduced or transmitted in any form or by any means, including informational storage and retrieval systems, without permission in writing from the author or publisher, except for brief quotations in a review.

Edited by Kristen Eckstein
Cover design by Joe Eckstein

Published by Jubilee! Press™, an imprint of Imagine! Books™
part of Imagine! Studios™
P. O. Box 547, Galloway, Ohio 43119
Email: contact@imaginestudiosonline.com
www.imaginestudiosonline.com

Published in Association with Ambassador Press, LLC
P. O. Box 722, Reynoldsburg, Ohio 43068-0722
Email: info@ambassadorpressllc.com
http://ambassadorpressllc.com

All scripture quotations, unless otherwise indicated, are taken from the *Holy Bible, New King James Version*®. Copyright © 1982 by Thomas Nelson, Inc. Used by permission. All rights reserved.

Scripture quotations marked (NIV) are taken from the *Holy Bible, New International Version*®. NIV®. Copyright©1973, 1978, 1984 by International Bible Society. Used by permission of Zondervan. All rights reserved.

Scripture quotations marked (KJV) are taken from the *Holy Bible, King James Version*

ISBN 0-9764353-3-0
Library of Congress Control Number: 2004118291

First Jubilee! Press paperback printing: March 2005

This book is dedicated to God, my Father, who first so loved me that He gave His Son, my Lord and Savior, who by his obedience gave his life, and in turn, gave the Holy Spirit,
His precious gift, to empower and to comfort
and to keep me for all eternity.

Contents

Introduction   *xiii*

Seasons of the Soul   *1*

    I Sing in My Garden   2
    The First Flower   3
    Sunrise   4
    Aubade   5
    One Red Rose   6
    The Old Oak Stump   7
    Autumn Sestina   8
    Witness   10
    Frosted Wood Scene   11
    Winter Solstice   12
    Summer Solstice   13
    Signs and Seasons: A Sestina   14
    Light of the World   16
    Time   18
    Seeds of Friendship   19
    The Eternal Moment   20
    Spring Green   21
    An Hundredfold   21
    Until Spring   22

In the Vernacular   *23*

    Why Don't Somebody Help Me Praise the Lord?   24
    My Madsong   26
    Songs Since   27
    Hand upon the Plow   29
    Good News Day   31
    We Be Brothers   32
    God's Armorbearers   33
    There Was a Time   34
    Homecoming   35
    A Gunnison Country Chris'mas   37
    The Wise Men   39
    No Mo Blues   40
    Final Victory   42

Stone Upon Stone

Ain't No Harm to Moan Sometime   44
Little Boy's Blues   45
Time Ain't Long   46
The Burden Bearer   47
New Name   48
Do It Now!   49

Golden Moments   51

Intimacy   52
The Essence of Your Presence   53
Before I Knew You   54
A Single Image   55
Peace   57
A Blush of Innocence   58
The Call   59
Sonneteer   60
Strengthened for the Journey   61
Oh, To See the Mystery   62
Fasting   63
The Teacher's Task   64
This Year of My Jubilee   65
The Way You Speak   66
Once I Built A Fire   67
Much More   68
More Than Metaphor   69
Just A Rehearsal   70

Psalms of Remembrance   71

Stone upon Stone: A Psalm of Remembrance   72
A Song of Celebration   75
The Song of Pentecost   76
Sunday Morning Glories   77
Taking It Personally   81
"And David Danced before the Lord with All His Might"   82
David Lee, Jr. has a conversation with a tree   83
Thanksliving   84
plainsong   85
Born for Luck   86
Your Life Is A Book   87
The Gift   88
Reading the Word of God: A Psalm of Preparation   90

Contents

    Try Me   92
    After the Art of the Apothecary   93
    Song of Triumph   94
    Enoch's Song   95
    Firstfruits   96
    "If the Lord tarries. . ."   97
    A Psalm of Endless Praise   98

About the Author   *101*

Then those who feared the LORD spoke to one another, and the LORD listened and heard them; so a book of remembrance was written before Him for those who fear the LORD and who meditate on His name.

"They shall be Mine," says the LORD of hosts, "On the day that I make then my jewels." And I will spare them as a man spares his own son who serves him."

Malachi 3:16, 17

Introduction

Stone upon Stone: Psalms of Remembrance is a collection of poetry inspired by the Book of Psalms and other passages of Scripture. My love for the Psalms of David goes back to my childhood days in Gary, Indiana. In the early 1950s I recall my memorizing the First Psalm, which I can still recite by heart. In Junior High I committed Psalm 27 to memory, and the words still pulsate from my soul. The words of that particular psalm, which has become my favorite, have been a special source of strength and comfort since the world-altering events of September 11, 2001.

Beyond my exposure to poetry through the Psalms, I was introduced to power of poetry in my freshman year of high school when Mrs. Frances Uncapher, my English teacher, read from *One Hundred Narrative Poems* with such ease and familiarity that I felt she knew each of the authors personally. In my junior year, Mrs. Hortense House required our English class to memorize two poems: "Barter" by Sara Teasdale, and "The Road Not Taken" by Robert Frost. More than forty years later I could still recite those works from memory and incorporated them into a number of composition and literature classes I have taught at Otterbein College.

In 1960 I enrolled as a freshman pharmacy student at Purdue University. In my freshman composition class, I inadvertently wrote a catalogue poem when I completed this in-class writing assignment: "May I Tell You What Delights Me?". Near the top of my list was the Book of Psalms.

Years later I recognized that poetic seeds had been sown in my college years. Fruit from the scattering of those seeds sown during the turbulent 1960s abound, even in this collection of poetry. In 1961 I just happened to notice a poster advertising a lecture on campus. Dr. Rosey Poole was going to present a lecture "Beyond the Blues", a discussion and reading of African American poetry. At the time I was a pharmacy major but thought this sounds interesting, and so I went just out of curiosity. She exposed the audience to a number of black poets. Aside from Phyllis Wheatley and Paul Laurence Dunbar, whose names I remembered having heard previously, most of the poets whom she mentioned were unknown to me. She sparked an interest in reading more of these and other poets, and two years later I took an oral interpretation course, and for my final presentation I put together a reading of works by African American poets.

Twenty-years later in 1981, I enrolled in the Ph.D. program at Indiana University, pursuing a doctorate in English with a minor in Afro-American Studies. I completed a dissertation in 1986 entitled "Portrait of the Bondslave in the Bible: Slavery and Freedom in the Works of Four Afro-American Poets." Three of those poets, I first heard of at that providential lecture in 1961. Today, more than forty years after my introduction to black poetry, I am a professor of African American literature and a published poet.

Introduction

My actual aspirations to write poetry occurred when I was drafted into the U.S. Army in January 1967. While I was a pharmacy instructor at the Medical Field Service School in San Antonio at Fort Sam Houston, Texas, I rode the crest of the Jesus Movement, a national revival impacting the lives of countless young people and others. I experienced a powerful conversion that introduced me to the transforming power of God through receiving the Holy Spirit and studying of the Bible.

I continued to write poetry once I was discharged from the Army in December 1968. In 1984 I published *Ears Near to the Lips of God*, some of whose works are revised and added to this manuscript. In 1994 I submitted a manuscript of poetry *Sacred Jazz: Music, Mood and Mind* to the Persephone Press Book Award, and it was published as the runner-up entry and republished in 1998. Four poems from that collection were also revised and appear in the current manuscript which takes its title from the poem inspired by a return visit to San Antonio in 1993 when I wrote "Stone upon Stone: A Psalm of Remembrance."

Stone upon Stone: Psalms of Remembrance is, for the most part, the fruit of my first sabbatical leave from Otterbein College during the fall quarter of 1999. A number of works have been added to the original manuscript of sixty-four poems completed in April 2000. The current collection of seventy-six poems is divided into four sections, each of which contains an introductory scripture. Most of the works have an epigraph or opening scripture or quotation or dedication.

In "Seasons of the Soul", the first section, I express my appreciation for the beauty of Nature and comment on the God's handiwork. "In the Vernacular" contains a number of dialect poems, revealing influences of Paul Laurence Dunbar, but they are written in more contemporary black speech. This section also features blues poetry, another form of African American poetry offered from my spiritual perspective. "Golden Moments" are reflective works inspired, in part, by the statement of Saint Augustine: "To contemplate the truth and to share the fruits of that contemplation." The final section, "Psalms of Remembrance", are recollections from childhood and beyond and songs of celebration of the goodness of God.

I would like to express my gratitude to those who have contributed to my life and with whom I share the success of this endeavor: To Otterbein College for providing the sabbatical leave program; to my wonderful wife, Brenda, and our two lovely daughters, Melissa and Angela, who have always been sources of inspiration, joy and blessing; to my mother, the late Jessie Marie Johnson, and my sister, Cheryl Thompson, two awesome women of faith who have touched my life; my mother-in-law, Rosa Lee McNary Williams, a fellow poet and wonderful woman of God; Pastors Eric and Carolyn Warren, my brother-in-law and sister-in-law, for our friendship and mutual joy in serving God (a number of these poems were inspired by Pastor Eric Warren's teachings from the Scriptures). These poems are also written in loving memory of my father, Lonnie Johnson; my father-in-law, Barney J. Warren, and my brother-in-law, Elliott Thompson, great men whose

Introduction

lives also influenced me. There are so many others, family members and friends, too numerous to name.

May these poems that overflow from the depths of my heart inspire all those who read them. May they resound with love, joy, and peace and reflect of the manifold wisdom of God.

Lonnell E. Johnson

Seasons of the Soul

"To everything there is a season, a time for every purpose under heaven."

Ecclesiastes 3:1

I Sing in My Garden

Oh, sing unto the LORD a new song!
Sing to the LORD, all the earth.
Sing to the LORD, bless his name;
Proclaim the good news from day to day.

Psalm 96:1–2

I sing in my garden and reap the good,
The bounty of living sixty-two years.
Each note seems to evoke a stream of tears
That fall, not because of some somber mood
But flow from a heart filled with gratitude.
The folksong of the farmer thrills my ears
Each time plowing, planting or harvest nears.
I compose my song, having understood
Lyrics I did not know when I was young,
When life was uncertain, my song unsure.
Now from my green garden I garner truth.
A song of conviction flows from my tongue.
I am seasoned and strengthened to endure,
Knowing the best lines are yet to be sung.

Seasons of the Soul

The First Flower

*Behold, I tell you a mystery;
We shall not all sleep, but we shall all be changed—
in a moment, in the twinkling of an eye,
at the last trumpet. For the trumpet shall sound,
and the dead will be raised incorruptible,
and we shall be changed.*

I Corinthians 15:51–52

As
the trumpet,
the first daffodil,
heralds the birth of Spring
today,

so
shall the shofar
sound golden notes
to take us unawares
someday.

Sunrise

The sun also arises, and the sun goes down,
and hastens to the place where it arose.

Ecclesiastes 1:5

Today I beheld the beauty
    of the dawning of the day,
the purple mountain majesty
    crowned with mounds of sifted snow
displayed against the molten sky.

I saw no veil, no morning mist.
    The sun's purest rays revealed
mountains of uncut amethyst
    ignited in dawn's afterglow,
lingering as a fading flame.

Fleeting embers are man's reward,
    tokens of passing pleasures till
we all are gathered with our Lord
    to see Him face to face and know
the sun shall rise to set no more.

Aubade

*Then God made two great lights:
the greater light to rule the day,
and the lesser light to rule the night.
He made the stars also.*

Genesis 1:16

Daybreak tiptoes with soft footfalls, floating
To still the silver trill of nocturne's flute.
Miss Moon in satin negligee begins
To blush with morn's first ray. Swiftly she veils
Her face with pink chiffon, and then she takes
To flight, embarrassed by the brazen light.
The daystar dons a robe of gold brocade
And crimson silk, designed to awe the soul.
The reigning queen ascends for me to see
The royal splendor of her grand debut.
Dawn tunes my heart to join in her aubade
And sing a lyric hymn of praise to God.

One Red Rose

"I am the rose of Sharon. . . ."

tender
reminder
love
grows

only
God knows
all the love
behind

one
red
rose

The Old Oak Stump

The grass withers, the flower fades,
because the breath of the LORD blows upon it:
surely the people are grass.
The grass withers, the flower fades,
but the word of our God stands for ever.
                                    Isaiah 40:7–8

I stand dead center on the old oak stump,
The ruin of a woodland monument,
My feet encircled by the woody rings
That number far beyond remembered years.
I read between the lines of annual
Reports a history of all you have seen:
You saw the Shawnee dance around his fires;
You knew the name of each German who came
To farm, to build, and to beget his sons
Under the shaded beauty of your boughs;
You spread your arms and offered shelter as
A dwelling place for bird and beast and boy.
Yet time's swift stroke condemned the tenement,
As progress served its eviction notice.
Men leveled the tree whose lease had expired,
Legend of a people, long since cut off,
Like meadow grass overgrowing the land
Where I see human nature's family tree:
Fleeting as baby's breath, man's day sprinkles
Grasslands for a season, then blows away.
All life evaporates like dew, except
The Word of God, which ever shall inspire.

Autumn Sestina

"Ho! Every one who thirsts, come to the waters;
and you who have no money, Come, buy, and eat.
Yes, come, buy wine and milk without money and without price.
Why do you spend money for what is not bread,
and your wages for what does not satisfy?
Listen carefully to me, and eat what is good,
and let your soul delight itself in abundance.

                           Isaiah 55:1–2

Acorns scatter and roll like coins of gold;
Leaves fly like silver dimes flung from a rich
Man's pouch to children who squander their wealth,
Counting the cobblestone clouds in the sky.
Deep rust and scarlet curtains dress the stage
Where trees change gowns on a warm autumn day.

The face of the sun clocks the short-term day
With reduced payments from its store of gold.
The sun keeps bankers' hours at this late stage
When precious daylight belongs to the rich
Who redeem the time from the gilded sky
And rise with the dawn to claim the sun's wealth.

Farmers fill their coffers with nature's wealth,
Collect rewards from summer's last full day,
Gather golden grain like rain from the sky.
Paths lined with silver dust and mums of gold
Lead to treasured fruit of the vine. So rich
Is the bounty of harvest at full stage.

Seasons of the Soul

Night falls as cameo moon takes the stage
Of the twilight show. Eyes assess the wealth
Of the opal pendant against the rich
Velvet backdrop at the close of the day.
Evening sun, like a pocketwatch of gold,
Slips into the vest of the dark-blue sky.

The sunset flickers and ignites the sky,
Like a glowing match before ember stage.
The warm days of autumn are scarce as gold
That flowed freely when Fall spent all her wealth.
Though she would lavish the land in her day,
Few will remember that this heiress was rich.

Those who invest precious dreams will be rich
When they look into the gray winter sky.
Those who hold tokens from Fall's gold leaf day,
Though they long for life in a greener stage,
Even in snow will be warmed by their wealth
And find full return in the Spring's new gold.

No one alive is rich enough to stage
An auction to buy sky and earth with wealth,
Yet the one who spends each day needs no gold.

Witness

Luke 24:1–9
The account of the women at the empty tomb

Though we did not journey with the women
In the dark before dawn that first day,
Nor were we walking, weeping with them when
Two angels spoke, nor did we hear them say,
"He is not here but risen as he said;
Recall that on the third day he should rise;
Why seek you the living among the dead?"
Though we did not see with our naked eyes,
In our hearts we know God's desire to bless.
Though we did not touch Christ nor did we see
The open tomb, yet we still bear witness.
We have a more sure word of prophecy.
By the spirit, fruit of our Promised Seed,
We surely know He is risen, risen, indeed.

Frosted Wood Scene

*Come now, and let us reason together, says the LORD,
though your sins be like scarlet, they shall be as white as snow;
though they are red like crimson, they shall be as wool.*

Isaiah 1:18

The stark nakedness
of the dark bark
blooms with crystal leaves.
Where death once reigned,
blossoms now flourish,
even as grace
did much more abound
and flower as
graceful almond trees.

I stand enraptured,
surrounded by
the fragile beauty
of the landscape
etched in a fuller
white than any
angel's bright raiment.

The frosted wood scene
shows God's design
to cleanse and make whole
the soul of man
that he might surely
know the pure love
that cleanses, covers
whiter than snow,
Lord, whiter than snow.

Winter Solstice

*And there will be signs in the sun; and in the moon,
and in the stars; and on the earth distress of nations,
with perplexity, the sea and the waves roaring;*

Luke 21:25

In the clear azure of the Eastern sky
Arises the winter solstice with its signs,
Marking out the shortest day of the year:
A full moonstone pin sets off Dawn's chiffon dress;
Like a sparkling diamond set in the ear,
A brilliant nova lingers to impress.
Wonders appear to those with eyes to see.
Out of darkness has emerged a great light,
Revealing a more sure word of prophecy.
Until the day star shall arise in our hearts,
Let us fix our eyes toward the Eastern sky
And look up, for our redemption draws nigh.
Let us not just see signs each season brings
But understand the meaning of these things.

Summer Solstice

*And so we have the prophetic word confirmed,
which you do well to heed as a light that shines
in a dark place, until the day dawns,
and the morning star rises in your hearts;*

II Peter 1:19

As a bright light shining in a dark place,
The morning star glows in the Eastern sky.
A crescent ring wanes to thinnest sliver
Before the new moon ascends to debut.
Spring's short-term lease has already expired
On the summer solstice, the longest day.
A total eclipse of the sun precludes
Righteousness and peace have kissed each other,
As bride and groom now sit in heavenly realms.
With the crimson dawning of this new day,
Transform me to be more than telescope.
Open my heart and so fashion a space,
A place prepared to receive the daystar,
As the Sun of righteousness shall arise
In glorious power with healing in his wings.
Open my eyes that I may see we have
An even more sure word of prophecy.

Signs and Seasons: A Sestina

Then God said, "Let there be lights in the firmament of the heavens to divide the day from the night; and let them be for signs, and for seasons, and for days, and years; And let them be for lights in the firmament of the heavens to give light upon the earth"; and it was so.

Genesis 1:14–15

The heavens declare the glory of God,
Creator of the sun, moon and each star,
Emblazened and christened and called by name,
Celestial bodies made for signs and seasons
When all the morning stars sang together
And all the sons of God shouted for joy.

A dirge descends to hush the shouts of joy:
Awesome lament in the presence of God.
All the angelic hosts strive together:
One third align with the first morning star;
Expelled to endure all earthly seasons,
Lucifer and those who defame God's name.

All things work to give glory to His name.
After days of mourning come days of joy,
Feast days to celebrate for all seasons
That the earth might know the goodness of God.
Observe the thin crescent and morning star:
Venus and the moon kiss and rise together.

Seasons of the Soul

Righteousness and truth have come together
In Jesus Christ, name above every name,
Grand debut of the bright and morning star:
Source of every blessing and endless joy.
The heavenlies reveal the mind of God
Displayed in stars to guide for all seasons.

Seedtime and harvest, sequence of seasons,
Reaping and sowing both come together
To unfold before us the plan of God,
To give glory and honor to His name
When midnight shall give birth to dawning joy
To ascend with the bright and morning star.

The shofar's call shall precede the day star.
Look up, observe the signs and the seasons:
Prelude to our measureless days of joy
When we all shall be gathered together;
Each knee shall bow; each tongue confess His name
Before the throne of the Almighty God.

Glory to God, who knows by heart each star.
We praise His name, now and for all seasons;
Together all creation shouts for joy.

Light of the World

> *"You are the light of the world. A city that is set on a hill cannot be hidden. Nor do men light a lamp, and put it under a basket, but on a lampstand; and it gives light to all who are in the house. Let your light so shine before men, that they may see your good works, and glorify your Father in heaven."*
>
> Matthew 5:14–16

A call comes ringing. . .

The light that from creation split the dark
still shines today. The same sun that once graced
Eden's green place still warms the earth each day.
Without the light there is no life, no hope
For growth, no power to live and give birth.
Without the light there is only the night
To swallow the land and smother all life.

Somewhere someone sits in darkness, crying. . .

Send the light. . .

The love of Christ constrains us to go forth,
To shine as beacons and carry the love,
To offer shelter from stormy places,
To light the path of everyone who longs
To be at home within God's family room.

Seasons of the Soul

Send the light...

With torch held high, let us stand upon the Rock:
    a lantern, a lampstand, a beacon, a lighthouse,
        a city set on a hill that cannot be hid

Let it shine...

Though the darkness thickens, let our lights so shine.
Let us speak God's Word and echo God's voice that
First spoke light into being, commanding it to shine

So let it shine...

        So let it shine...

                So let it shine...

                      forever more.

Time

> *So teach us to number our days,*
> *that we may gain a heart of wisdom.*
>
> Psalm 90:12

Our lives begin with a handful of coins.
To wisely invest or squander each dime
The daily choice, though the Bible enjoins
Us to walk as wise, to redeem the time,
As a wise buyer with talents would keep
His eye on best buys sought before the chime
Should ring to bring each soul to his brief sleep
Or those who remain shall be gathered to
The bosom of the Father, there to reap
Their rewards, as each shall receive his due.
Time is fixed; we cannot borrow nor lend.
The coins we are given seem far too few.
Life is the sum of the coins that we spend
Before our time in life's market shall end.

Seeds of Friendship

*Let love be without hypocrisy.
Abhor what is evil. Cling to what is good.
Be kindly affectionate to one another with brotherly love,
in honor giving preference to one another;*

Romans 12:9–10

There is a special place,
a space where warm eyes meet,
where hearts entwine
as friends embrace.

Hand-in-hand,
we have walked that land
and glimpsed the vistas
of God's plan:
a foretaste of the place
where peace unfolds
and love abounds,
where golden moments never end.

The seeds of friendship we have sown
shall bloom and abound in our minds
to offer us fragrant bouquets
to flourish in our garden spot.

Though we travel far from our home,
distance cannot dissolve the bond:
the love of God that never fails
has sealed our hearts
to make us one.

The Eternal Moment

Redeeming the time, because the days are evil.
                              Ephesians 5:16

Now is always the time.

Though grains of sand
fall and form
a mountain
range,

Now
does not
add nor take;
the moment cannot change.

The time is always **Now**.

Spring Green

Psalm 23

Grass green hillsides arch
and flow toward a quiet stream
where rest newborn lambs.

A Hundredfold

*But others fell on good ground, sprang up,
and yielded a crop a hundredfold. . . .*

Luke 8:8a

Orchards of pomegranate trees
stem from fruit of a single seed
whose life is found within itself,
sown in fertile soil of the heart.

Until Spring

So when this corruptible has put on incorruption,
and this mortal has put on immortality,
then shall be brought to pass the saying that is written,
"Death is swallowed up in victory. O Death,
where is your sting? O Hades, where is your victory?

I Corinthians 15:54–55

Whether on earth or shuttled in the sky,
Death snuffs out our candles in devious ways,
For each man must learn to number his days,
Although the soul still probes to fathom why.
The mind made numb with pain can only try
To make sense of the immense ache that stays.
The answer sounds since Adam but still dismays:
It is appointed unto man once to die.
Though grief surrounds us, comfort can be shown.
The sun melts frost with new life as surely
As blossoms will flourish from seeds once sown.
Until Spring, on tip-toe I yearn to see
The day when I shall know as I am known,
When death is swallowed up in victory.

In the Vernacular

*He has put a new song in my mouth—Praise to our God.
Many will see it and fear and will put their trust in the Lord.*
                                                   Psalm 40:3

Stone Upon Stone

Why Don't Somebody Help Me Praise the Lord?

Psalm 107

When I was down so low
    it looked like up to me,
You broke those heavy chains
    and gave me sweet liberty.

Why Don't Somebody Help Me Praise the Lord?

When I was so big and bad,
    tryin to be my own man,
You opened my blinded eyes
    and then showed me *Your* master plan.

Why Don't Somebody Help Me Praise the Lord?

I was headin straight to hell,
    And I was goin in grand style
But you picked me up, turnt me round,
    And you caused me to think awhile.

Why Don't Somebody Help Me Praise the Lord?

Stumblin down the road of life,
    I was wastin all my youth,
Then took a right turn to Jesus Christ;
    Now I'm walkin the path of truth.

Why Don't Somebody Help Me Praise the Lord?

In the Vernacular

You couldn't tell me nothin
    bout nothin I hadn't seen or heard,
Then I ran right smackdab into
    the power of God's matchless Word.

    Why Don't Somebody Help Me Praise the Lord?

With lovin arms you reach way down
    And snatched me from Satan's outhouse,
Sought me and flat-out rescued me,
    Fixed me up in my Father's house.

    Why Don't Somebody Help Me Praise the Lord?

For mighty peace like a river
    washin away confusion and strife,
What can I give you in return?
    Yes, Sir, I'll give you back my life.

    Why Don't Somebody Help Me Praise the Lord?

My Madsong

We are fools for Christ's sake,
but you are wise in Christ!
We are weak, but ye are strong!
You are distinguished, but we are dishonored.

                        I Corinthians 4:10

I am stark raving mad as a gitsy;
I am insane and crazy as a loon.
    Though my voice is stronger,
    My lyrics are wronger.
My madsong is plainly out of tune
(But all the while I smile).

I am a rare and bizarre exception
Who loves to laugh outloud and cry.
    My mind borders hysterical;
    Each day I see a miracle.
I live on earth with my home in the sky
(And all the while I smile).

I make my point with certainty—
Another fact which clearly shows
    That I am deceived or naiver,
    With the mind of a child, a believer
Who knows that he knows that he knows
(Why all the while I smile).

In the Vernacular

    So I still dream my dreams and live
    My life in such a simple style.
        The world wants to eat me for supper,
        But I just laugh and keep the upper
    Hand and keep walking mile by mile
    (As all the while I smile).

    They call me kook, fanatic and fool
    Because of my peculiar knack.
        Folks think me still odder
        Because I talk with God, my Father,
    And furthermore, yes, He talks back
    (And all the while I smile).

Songs Since

Oh, sing to the LORD a new song!
For he has done marvelous things;
His right hand and his holy arm
have gained Him the victory.

                        Psalm 98:1

My mobile mind recalls all the witty
Songs I've heard since I first began to talk,
Every childhood rhyme and infant ditty,
Such silly nonsense sounds of jabberwock.

I remember in my boppin doo-wop days
When I was no more than a high school lad,
I dug the D.J.'s sound that seldom stays—
Oldies but goodies, old and good, so bad.

Stone Upon Stone

Some of my songs I sang before I knew
Any of the reasons to cherish them,
Of simple black people, humble and who
Drank in renewed strength from their vintage hymn.

Then came *chansons d'amour,* delights to learn,
Filled with delicate words I wished I'd penned,
Lightly descend like dew upon a fern,
Lovely lyrics to share with special friend.

Each kind of music seems to mirror me,
Express all of my innermost hopes and joys,
Reflect my soulful *melancholody*
Ennobled by the rich chords' counterpoise.

All is a song, a noted writer said,
And I too sing my song and hold no strife.
Instead of a just a dirge drummed for the dead,
I sing a mighty melody of life.

In the Vernacular

Hand upon the Plow

"Keep your hand on the plow, hold on!"
—Black Spiritual

When life ain't like it spose to be,
Right then and there it occurs to me
Folks been in fixes worse than me,
Right in the Bible where I see:

The Lord will make a way somehow.
Just keep your hand upon the plow.

Pharaoh said, "Kill each Hebrew boy,"
But Moses' Ma was full of joy
Cause Pharaoh's daughter raised *her* boy.
The Lord will make a way somehow.

The lions looked so lean and thin
When they throwed Daniel in the den,
But Old Man Daniel didn't bend.
Just keep your hand upon the plow.

Stone Upon Stone

When Jesus died, God paid the cost
And at that time all seem like lost,
But God planned ahead for Pentecost.
The Lord will make a way somehow.

Paul and Silas didn't rant and wail
When they throwed both of them in jail.
They called on God, and He didn't fail.
Just keep your hand upon the plow.

When troubles start to buggin you
Remember, there's just one thing to do:
Look to God and He'll see you through.
What he did for them, He'll do for you.

The Lord will make a way somehow.
Just keep your hand upon the plow.

In the Vernacular

Good News Day

*This is the day the LORD has made;
we will rejoice and be glad in it.*

Psalm 118:24

It's a good new day
    no blues day
    new shoes
    no way to lose
What a good new day

It's a great day
    I can't wait day
    lift your voice
    let's rejoice
Good God, a good news day

It's a payday
    goin my way day
    no nay—all yea
    what you say
Such a good news day

It's a live it up day
    overflowin cup day
    It's a bright and bubbly
    doubly lovely
Show-nuff good news day

We Be Brothers

*"Spirit is thicker than blood.
Oh, yes, it is, brother."*

Skip Mesquite
songwriter, saxophonist

men born again in brotherhood
beyond thin skinship of the soul
not blood but spirit makes us kin
we be true brothers, brother-man

I dig your gig, so rap to me
and play the sounds I need to hear
tune me in and play my number
just call me on your saxophone

soothe my soul with those mellow notes
flowing from your horn of plenty
man, make your heartsong melt my dark
and paint my skies in sunrise hues

I can escape the basement gloom
to scale the palace stairs with you
we climb to where the air is rare
we be true brothers, brother-man

In the Vernacular

God's Armorbearers

for Eric L. Warren

My Brother...

When all is said and done, we must confess:
"Armorbearers" is what we spose to be.
But men of God today don't wear that mess.
Swords, shields, and spears are weapons we don't see.
In this case, we read God's Word and then try
To make sense of this Old Testament phrase,
To see just how it begins to apply
To living in these last and evil days.
We want to find words to put on this page;
From the depths of our hearts we must convey
Words that speak loudly to this present age.
In response, this is all we have to say:
"We won't take no jive and don't cut no slack—
God's Armorbearers Pledge: We got ya back!"

My Brother...

There Was a Time

*Remember now your Creator in the days of your youth,
before the difficult days come, and the years draw near,
when you say, "I have no pleasure in them":*

Ecclesiastes 12:1

There was a time when he rejoiced,
Would testify before the saints
His only joy in Jesus Christ
And preach the Word with no restraints.

How he could pray, oh, way you say!
He'd lead the service every week
And sweep the folk from storefront floors
And lead them to the mountain peak.

One day he climbed the churchyard fence
And sampled fruit from other trees,
Tasted ologies and isms,
Alluring sweetness of degrees.

The life he had never questioned
Was challenged every day at school
From the pressures and the pleasures
His white-hot fire for God turned cool.

Now when the churchfolk gather round
Each week, they sing and pray and moan.
They pray their wayward, long lost son,
Will someday find his way back home.

In the Vernacular

Homecoming

The Parable of the Prodigal Son
Luke 15:11–32

I prodigalled
and partied
and boogied my
nights away.

I humped and bumped
and stumbled
till I found myself
in a ditch.

I squandered all
of my bread,
down to my
very last crumb.

I had no friends
to turn to
I had no place to go
but home.

I tried to sneak back
unnoticed,
but Daddy ran
to meet me
and greet me with
open arms
(like I'd been down
the road apiece,
or just got
back from town,

Stone Upon Stone

or never been
gone at all).

He didn't ask me
where I'd been,
didn't ask how
much I'd spent.

He forgave me,
just forgot
all the times I'd
plumb missed the mark.

He spread the
welcome table
and had a
family feast
to satisfy
my hunger
and meet my
every need.

Later on in the
midnight peace
when Pa and I
were alone,
we said nothing,
yet so much;
then through tears
of joy he said,

"It's all right, son—
it's all right, now."

In the Vernacular

A Gunnison Country Chris'mas

Ask me to choose the best time of the year,
My most fav'ritest time of all. This must
Be my choice, for nothin' on earth even comes near
The heart of a Gunnison Country Chris'mas.

My heart beats fast when I think of it now:
All the things our fam'ly use to do;
Ma'd be a fixin', teachin' the girls how
To get all the cookin done. I'd help too;
Pa and me'd go and chop the Chris'mas tree.
We'd all trim it with ornaments we'd make:
Carved wood and calico bows, cute as can be.
There'd be somethin; for everyone to take
And put on the tree. A white star was hung
Way up on top. The sweet pine boughs was draped
With popcorn and cranberries that we'd strung.
There'd be lots of surprises 'cause Pa'd scraped
And saved to buy all the kids a nice gift.
Chris'mas was a time to give, yes, indeed,
A special time that never fails to lift
Your heart to share with other folk in need.
The good Lord had blessed us with so much more
Than we could rightly use, so we would share
With the men in the jailhouse and the poor,
Who were pleased to know that some folk still care.
Those were very special times I recall,
The best times in the world, for goodness sakes,
The laughin' and carryin' on and all
The food you et until your belly aches.
To start things off, the men proposed a toast:
"Here's to the ladies" and "to Pa's good wine."
Then we'd sing the songs we all loved the most,

Stone Upon Stone

"The Star-spangled Banner," fav'rite of mine.
Buck and the boys like eatin' the best.
You'd think they hadn't et in ten days.
Ma'd start the ox-tail soup, then bring on the rest:
Salmon and trout, along with the big trays
Full of pheasant and beef and sav'ry meats:
Venison, buffalo stewed in a pot;
Plus 'tatas, beans and rice, squashes and beets,
With elk, hare, and quail—all the game Pa'd shot.
But that wa'n't all; then come sweet treats to boot.
On this one day, your stomach was big as your eyes.
There was nuts and hard candy, raisins and fruit.
Apple, currant, mincemeat—all kinds of pies.
We'd make the most of Chris'mas cause we knew real well
This was the last big shindig 'fore winter set in.
Old folks and young 'uns would square off and dance a spell,
Knowin' this was the last chance they'd be gettin'.
Seem like we didn't have nary a worry
In this simple life we was livin'.
When Pa would read us the Chris'mas story
'Bout the greatest gift that's ever been given.
That was my fav'ritest time, without a doubt,
As I think back on them mountaintop days.
Ain't that what Chris'mas spose to be all about?
Just bless and be blessed in so many ways.

Ask me to choose the best time of the year,
My most fav'ritest time of all. This must
Be my choice, for nothin' on earth even comes near
The heart of a Gunnison Country Chris'mas.

In the Vernacular

The Wise Men

Matthew 2:1–12

Men of wisdom from the East
    looked for the King of Kings,
saw his star when he was born
    and traveled countless miles.

They did not seek a stable,
    nor did they seek a throne,
but the bright star led them to
    a house in Nazareth.

Here they beheld the man-child
    to someday reign as king
and opened up their treasures:
    gold, frankincense, and myrrh.

Men of wisdom of today
    no longer seek a child.
wise men seek the Savior's face
    and long to make Him Lord.

Men of wisdom of today
    still journey far to share.
They bear the rarest gift of all—
    the meekness of a seeking heart.

No Mo Blues

*You have turned for me my mourning
into dancing; You have put off my sackcloth,
and clothed me with gladness;*

Psalm 30:11

I use to be a big-time blues singer
In the union for singers of the blues.
I use to be a big-time blues singer
In the union for singers of the blues,
But I turnt in my union card,
Ain't gonna pay no mo union dues.

When I was a full-time blues singer,
Doin whatsonever I choose—
When I was a full-time blues singer,
Doin whatsonever I choose—
Drinkin and smokin and messin round
I was payin my blues singer's dues.

When I use to sing the low-down blues,
I could show-nuff cry and croon.
When I use to sing the low-down blues,
I could show-nuff cry and croon.
Then I met my precious Jesus,
Now I'm hummin a brand new tune.

In the Vernacular

　　　　　I gotta go find my agent
　　　　　And tell him, "Say, Man, you been fired!"
　　　　　I gotta go find my agent
　　　　　And tell him, "Say, Man, you been fired!"
　　　　　Since I met my precious Jesus,
　　　　　This old blues singer's done retired.

　　　　　I'm gonna tell everybody,
　　　　　I want the whole world to see.
　　　　　I'm gonna tell everybody,
　　　　　I want the whole world to see.
　　　　　I just gotta testify
　　　　　What my precious Jesus done for me.

　　　　　The day He stepped into my heart,
　　　　　The sun shined in my front door.
　　　　　The day He stepped into my heart,
　　　　　The sun shined in my front door.
　　　　　And since I met my precious Jesus,
　　　　　I ain't gonna sing the blues no mo.

Final Victory

I Corinthians 15:53–57
Romans 8:37–39

Old man crab is mighty sneaky,
    always creepin and up to no good,
Old man crab, is mighty sneaky,
    always creepin and up to no good,
That low-down dirty rascal,
    Messin with folk all round the neighborhood.

One dark day old man crab came callin,
    Crawlin in like some uninvited mouse,
One dark day old man crab came callin,
    Crawlin in like some uninvited mouse,
That nasty dirty devil,
    Sneakin in the back door of my sister's house.

First you first attacked my mama, old man crab,
    You tried to pinch her with your greatest fears,
First you first attacked my mama, old man crab,
    You tried to pinch her with your greatest fears,
But she didn't want no she-crab soup,
    You tried to served with pain and bitter tears.

You may have come to our house, old man crab,
    But I'm sorry, you can't stay.
You may have come to our house, old man crab,
    But I'm sorry, you can't stay.
Whatsonever in the world you may do,
    Everyday we still gonna watch, fight, and pray.

In the Vernacular

    Nothin' low down on earth, old man crab,
        Or nothin high up in heaven above,
    Nothin' low down on earth, old man crab,
        Or nothin high up in heaven above,
    Not even death, your creepin pardner,
        Can ever separate us from God's love.

    So git out my face, old man crab,
        I got your number, don't you see.
    So git out my face, old man crab,
        I got your number, don't you see.
    You may win this li'l biddy battle,
        But we show-nuff got the final victory.

    Some say our Savior's comin in the mornin;
        Some say in the midnight hour or high noon
    Some say our Savior's comin in the mornin;
        Some say in the midnight hour or high noon
    I got a feelin He's comin back
        To gather us together soon . . . and very soon.

Stone Upon Stone

Ain't No Harm to Moan... Sometime

a blues sonnet of sorts

A time to weep, and a time to laugh;
a time to mourn, and a time to dance;
                              Ecclesiastes 3:4

Jesus, the Savior said, "Blessed are they that mourn."
Yes, sir, the Master said, "Blessed are they that mourn."
Think about that the next time you're sad and forlorn.

Though you be a witness, proclaiming the gospel news.
Yes, you may be a witness, proclaiming the gospel news.
Yet and still, all God's children gotta taste the blues.

Hard times come—some folk have few, and some have many.
Hard times come—some folk have few, and some have many.
Don't forget, even Jesus had His Gethsemane.

Though dark clouds hang so low you don't know what to do,
Though dark clouds hang so low you don't know what to do,
Remember, the sun shines on the other side of "through."

Don't matter how low you go, how high you climb,
I declare, "Ain't no harm to moan... sometime."

In the Vernacular

Little Boy's Blues

a blues sonnet

Lord, may I learn never to frustrate your grace.
Lord, may I learn never to frustrate your grace.
May you never say to me, "Boy, Git out my face!"

May I honor and obey: let me be the one.
May I honor and obey: let me be the one.
May you always say to me, "Seek my face, my son."

I just can't grasp your ways, no matter how I try.
I just can't grasp your ways, no matter how I try.
You never scold but smile each time I ask you, "Why?"

Lord, may I never bring you shame or disgrace.
Lord, may I never bring you shame or disgrace.
Let me always run and hide in your secret place.

I'm show nuff a winner—ain't no way I can lose.
Everytime I cry, you hear this little boy's blues.

Stone Upon Stone

Time Ain't Long

(One Mo Blues Sonnet)

Say, Brother, "What in the world is going on?"
Say, Sister, "What in the world is going on?"
Seem like the love of God has long since up and gone.

Folks betraying ones they love, committing all sorts of crimes.
Folks betraying ones they love, committing all sorts of crimes.
The Bible says there show shall come perilous times.

Rather than receive a blessing, some folk take a curse.
Rather than receive a blessing, some folk take a curse.
Men and women show is waxing worse and worse.

Seem like folk enjoy flaunting they downright ugly ways.
Seem like folk enjoy flaunting they downright ugly ways.
These just gotta be the last and evil days.

So, I been thinking hard and it seems to me,
No, time ain't nearly long as it use to be.

In the Vernacular

The Burden Bearer

> *Glory, Glory, Hallelujah,*
> *When I lay my burden down.*

I stumbled up the rugged road;
I almost fell beneath the load
And spurned the pain inside my head,
Recalling words of one who
      "*Come unto me, and I will give you rest.*"

The yoke I bear cannot compare
With all he took upon Himself:
All sins, disease, and guilt, despair
That I could not forebear myself.

His burden was not made of wood,
His cross beyond all words can name.
Have I resisted unto blood?
Could I for joy endure such shame?

From a glimpse into his face
I'm strengthened by a second wind;
My mind's renewed to keep the pace
The load is lightened by my friend.

> *I feel better, so much better*
> *since I laid my burden down.*

Stone Upon Stone

New Name

*He who has an ear, let him hear what the Spirit
says unto the churches. To him that overcomes
I will give to eat of the hidden manna,
and will give him a white stone, and in the stone
a new name written, which no man knows
except him that receives it.*

        Revelation 2:17

More than a moniker,
a sobriquet attached
to the bridal bouquet,
a new name to change
or not, hyphenate,
ignore, keep, or discard
like outdated his and her towels;
how to handle this essence of being,
my new identity.

Like the trickster,
who tried to run his game
and get over on Jehovah
when he wrestled out a blessing
from the evening till the break of day,
I woke up one morning
with a new name and a gimp leg
to remind me of that all-night-face-to-face encounter
  when I sang
  "I told Jesus, be all right if He changed my name."

In the Vernacular

Do It Now!

*Redeeming the time, because the days are evil.
Therefore do not be unwise, but understanding
what the will of the Lord is.*

Ephesians 5:15–16

If you want to live each minute
With the fullest measure in it,
To run your best race and win it,
Then start to do it now!

Don't wait until it's tomorrow
To look for the time to borrow,
For you may be filled with sorrow
Unless you do it now!

Don't wait until the time is right.
By then you may have long lost sight
Of work to do with all your might.
Be sure to do it now!

Make up your mind; don't hesitate.
Now is the time to act, don't wait.
You've got nothing to lose; go straight
Ahead and do it now!

Just put the past behind somehow
And with each moment make a vow:
Now is the time to do it now.
Get up and do it now!

Golden Moments

How precious to me are your thoughts, O God!
How vast is the sum of them!

Were I to count them, they would outnumber the grains of sand.
When I awake, I am still with you.

                              Psalm 139:17,18 (NIV)

Intimacy

*You are my hiding place; you shall preserve me from trouble;
you shall surround me with songs of deliverance.*

                                      Psalm 32:7

Flood my blood with love and remove all fear.
Fulfill this yielded vessel, clothe me and
Draw me closer, nearer than breath or tear.
Share with me the intimacy you planned
For man to cherish and enjoy before
You fashioned earth or gave to man his form.
Whisper divine secrets hidden in store
Within your heart, my shelter from life's storm.
Fill my ears with words of peace that shall bring
Forth my lifelong song in your melody
That I may vocalize your will and sing
In one accord, in perfect harmony.
More intimate than friend or kin or wife
Is close-knit love God weaves within my life.

The Essence of Your Presence

You will show me the path of life:
in Your presence is fullness of joy;
at Your right hand there are pleasures
forevermore.

Psalm 16:11

The essence of your presence leaves behind
Dew distilled from a wisp of white muguet,
Lingering to perfume the rooms of my mind
With fresh-scented memories of a bouquet
Sent for no reason, only to show love.
A honeyed aftertaste stays on my lips.
Shekinah glory descends from above,
Touching secret places with fingertips.
In my inner ear plays a melody;
Whispered lyrics resound to let me know
A measure of the deep love shared with me.
I bask in splendor in the afterglow.
My spirit overflows and floods each sense,
While savoring the essence of your presence.

Before I Knew You

for my beloved Brenda

I thought of you long before I ever knew you.
When through the mist I beheld your lovely face.
Before our two lives touched, my heart reached out to you.

I could not speak your name, yet somehow I knew you
Would be all I could desire in style and grace.
I thought of you long before I ever knew you.

Alone, I saw the sunset, told myself you too
Needed a dearest friend to share this special place.
Before our two lives touched, my heart reached out to you.

Alone, I passed the time and asked myself who you
Were dreaming of, yet still longing to embrace
I thought of you long before I ever knew you.

I yearned to give my life, to share my soul with you
Who would make me feel whole and fill my empty space.
Before our two lives touched, my heart reached out to you.

God stretched out his hand, and then He gently drew you
To me with a true love that time cannot erase.
I thought of you long before I ever knew you.
Before our two lives touched, my heart reached out to you.

A Single Image

*For this reason shall a man leave
his father and mother,
and be joined to his wife,
and the two shall become one flesh.*

　　　　　　　　　　Ephesians 5:31

look upon the
mirror of our
soul
and
see
a
single image

one heart
wearing no
ill will

one mouth
speaking peace
and promises
fulfilled

one hand
bearing
only love
open
outstretched
toward you

Stone Upon Stone

we stand
before you
naked
unafraid
and free

there is
no fear
in love
so why
should we

we are His
He is one
so are we

one
plus
one
makes
one
in
word
in
deed
in
truth

Golden Moments

Peace

E'n la sua volontade e nostra pace[†]

Dante

Lord, make me an instrument of your peace I pray,
That from my life may stream heavenly melodies.
As consummate virtuoso compose and play
Upon my soul, inspire glorious harmonies.
In such measured moments of sweetest quietude,
Arrange serenades of praise. Let grace notes resound,
As my life crescendos in songs of gratitude,
Flowing from your heart, where grace and mercy abound.
Orchestrate aubades, nocturnes, songs at eventide;
Complete cantatas of peace within me, align
My desires and your pleasure. Here we abide,
Saxophone and soloist, communing by design.
Knowing my purpose, I remain quiet and still,
Composed in perfect peace, the center of His will.

[†]"In His will is our peace."
Paradiso, Canto III, l. 85

A Blush of Innocence

for Melissa and Angela

A blush of innocence upon the face
Of a budding girl at a tender age
Is the rare reward of those who trace
The essence of youth to its purest stage.
The heart of a child is an open garden
Where the rarest of flowers flourish and grow,
Though time schemes and devises to harden
The heart with weeds and walls that hide the glow.
Pure innocence blooms in a young girl's eyes.
Look upon her glowing face and cherish
The petals, the bud where such beauty lies,
For fruit shall come and the blossom perish.
Though beauty spans beyond adolescence,
No smile outshines a blush of innocence.

The Call

I, therefore, the prisoner of the Lord,
beseech you to walk worthy of the calling
with which you were called,

                                Ephesians 4:1

The call resounds like a repeated name
From the lips of a dear friend who knows you.
I clearly hear my name and see the flame
That lights the path of those whom God foreknew
Would hear and heed a higher destiny.
This calling only God can verify.
My ear cannot hear; my eye cannot see;
Yet within my heart I cannot deny
That I have heard and seen what few will know.
I must arise and strive to reach the place
Where the rivers of understanding flow
And never doubt God's purpose and His grace.
I stand in the unbroken line of all
Those who, having heard, rise to heed the call.

Sonneteer

*For it is God who works in you
both to will and to do for His good pleasure.*
       Philippians 2:13

Of the great works poets have penned, I find
The lilting sonnets of a bygone age,
Those words that all but sear the printed page,
Kindle candescent thoughts within my mind,
Exquisite phrasing of the bard gone blind
Whose context and syntax always engage
My heart to strive to earn the poet's wage.
But wasted words and thick phrasing remind
Me that I seek to write within my time.
Sometimes my words ring hollow as a thin
Tin cup. Yet I have joy far more sublime
Than all acclaim famed poets ever win.
Words may fail, but this sonneteer will rhyme
Now that I know God works and wills within.

Golden Moments

Strengthened for the Journey

*Wait on the LORD: be of good courage,
and he shall strengthen your heart;
wait, I say, on the LORD!*

Psalm 27:14

Let us pause to reflect upon the past,
Not with longing to relive bygone days.
Though some were fine, such moments cannot last
A lifetime. The budding rose never stays
The same but unfolds in lovelier ways.
Let us linger to absorb the essence
Of this moment's triumph. Another phase
Of growth we note within our lifetime since
We first began the quest toward excellence.
Let us look ahead with vision and strive
Toward greater goals, for each day we commence
To grow toward our perfection, as we thrive.
May we see clearly where our paths have led
And be strengthened for the journey ahead.

Oh, To See the Mystery

Ephesians 3

Enlighten my eyes that I might openly see;
Expand my mind and widen my comprehension
To understand the temple of the mystery.
Teach me to fully comprehend each dimension
And ascertain the magnitude without measure:
Reveal to me the true length,
>   though it is endless;
Teach me to find the full breadth,
>   though it is boundless;
Help me to reach the vast height,
>   though it is measureless;
Teach me to probe the great depth,
>   though it is fathomless.

Show me your divine design for the inner man.
Make plain the purpose, the pattern, the symmetry
Unfolded in the blueprints of your master plan
For the One Body, temple of awesome beauty.
Share with me the value of this priceless treasure,
The riches of the glory of this mystery
Held in the secret places of your good pleasure.
Take my hand and lead me, as you would guide a youth,
A son who lives to explore the depths of your truth.

Fasting

Isaiah 58

To fast, to abstain, to go without food,
To prostrate myself that You might find me
Stripped of pride and clothed in humility.
To focus on God, having understood
The motives evoking this solemn mood:
Heart-broken and open, yielding to be
Poured out before You a vessel, empty,
Ever striving to reach the highest good.
You alone have power to bless, refresh
And satisfy the thirsting of my heart,
To feed the inner hunger of my soul
And to fulfill the passions of my flesh.
Quenching the secret desire of each part,
Fasting reveals my yearning to be whole.

The Teacher's Task

For all those called to teach

The smallest spark can kindle a desire,
Ignite a fire to stir and warm the heart,
And through the years the embers from that fire
Will glow with light inflamed from that same start.
In the dark of night should a doubt arise,
A question of the road less traveled by,
Recall that same glow in a student's eyes
Shall dispel the chill of questioning why.
You who labored in the classroom have learned
That rapport with student, colleague and friend
Offers recompense beyond wages earned.
You who loved the teacher's task we commend:
May joy warm your heart and sustain you yet,
With memories of success and no regret.

Golden Moments

This Year of My Jubilee

Exodus 21:1–6
Leviticus 25:1–17

I stand alone clothed only with the wind
At the end of my seventh sabbath year.
Gathering of blessings now flow through my mind
As the shofar's call resounds in my ear
To proclaim this year of my jubilee.
I reflect upon the wonders of this grace
Wherein I stand, a bondslave now made free.
In this golden moment as I embrace
The truth and pledge to love as you command,
Pierce my ear—place your brand upon my soul.
Enlighten me so I may understand
That to run to serve is life's highest goal.
Unfold before me pleasures of your ways
And seal my vows to serve you all my days.

The Way You Speak

*So the LORD spoke to Moses face to face,
as a man speaks to his friend...*

Exodus 33:11a

Open my ears to do more than just hear
Your voice but also teach me to listen,
Though the flow of tears at times may glisten
My face. Teach me to recognize those clear,
Familiar words you whisper in my ear.
As my teacher, help me not to hasten
Each lesson, even the times you chasten,
While reassuring and holding me near.
In seeking to dwell in your hiding place,
My deepest yearning is to understand,
As I listen to hear each word you say.
Even as Moses knew you face to face,
So I long to know the way you speak and
Not question nor doubt but only obey.

Golden Moments

Once I Built A Fire

For our God is a consuming fire.
Hebrews 12:29

Scout's honor—Once I built a fire from scratch:
Gathered dried grass, spindly twigs, kindling and
A love letter, then proceeded as planned.
The careless wind brought me to my last match.
I held my breath and prayed this time it would catch,
Then knelt, exhaled, coaxing with bellows mild
As baby's breath to inspire my ailing child.
Throughout the night I lie awake and watch.
Indeed, I did my duty to protect,
To build and gather even more to give
To nourish this infant and not neglect,
For no fire has power within itself to live.
Though ablaze, fire demands not less but more.
Once from scratch I built a fire—Scout's honor.

Much More

*His lord said to him, "Well done,
good and faithful servant;
you have been faithful over a few things,
I will make you ruler over many things:
enter into the joy of your lord."*

Matthew 25:23

More than mere status or the embrace of the crown
Around the head or glory, honor or renown;
More than medals of gold or laurels that fade
With the thundering applause and ceaseless accolade;
More than any crowning achievement or success
Or the rarest prizes eyes could ever witness;
More than the taste of victory every time you try:
Such alluring sweetness can never satisfy.
So much more are these words when the race is finally
    won,
When we finish the course and cross the finish line,
And stand upon the *bema* where we shall incline
Our ears to hear God say, "Good and faithful servant,
    well done."
We shall bask in ultimate ecstasy of victory
And savor the goodness of God for all eternity.

Golden Moments

More Than Metaphor

Paul, a bondservant of Jesus Christ, called to be an apostle, separated to the gospel of God

Romans 1:1

To capture my essence I strive to find a word,
Phrase, image or mind picture to bring clarity,
To express my deep yearning for intimacy.
Like Paul, my calling card reads: "servant of the Lord."
Each fiber of my being and each emotion
Pulsates with lifeblood flowing from a servant's heart.
As I endeavor to learn and live to impart
The joy of serving with pure-hearted devotion,
I pledge to work in voluntary servitude,
As I fix my eyes, looking unto my Lord's hands,
To heed His Word and to do more than He commands,
To serve with love from a heart filled with gratitude.
Beyond a single concept, more than metaphor
Is this branded bondslave, who embodies "the more."

Just A Rehearsal

Early this morning before the light of day,
Before the first ray opened the door of night,
I could see the glory of the morning star:
A sapphire set upon a velvet pillow.
Saturn arises to beckon us homeward
Where the Bright and Morning Star shall then solo,
And all the sons of God again shout for joy.
Now our God invites us to join the chorus,
But to prepare we must learn our lines by heart,
As we audition on earth for various parts.
With enlightened eyes of understanding,
We now look up with a heavenly view,
Reminded, "This is just a rehearsal.
When we get to heaven, we'll really sing!"

Psalms of Remembrance

*Let the word of Christ dwell in you richly in all wisdom;
teaching and admonishing one another in psalms and hymns and
spiritual songs, singing with grace in your hearts to the Lord*

Colossians 3:16

Stone upon Stone: A Psalm of Remembrance

> *Now, let us all go back,*
> *back to the old landmark.*
> —Traditional Black Gospel Song

Half my life ago, marveling in your glory,
I reveled in the ecstasy of your presence
and thrilled to the gentle rhapsody of your voice,
as a naked child at play in the summer rain,
drenched in the flowing of the spirit's outpouring.
Now I return to reflect upon my journey
along the path leading to this present moment.
With quicksilver memories of those turbulent years,
here in this hallowed silence I raise my praisesong:
"How I got over! How I got over, My Lord!
My soul looks back and wonders how I got over."
From twelve stones of remembrance I build an altar—

El-Beth-el—stone upon stone I build this altar.

For a foundation, laid a precious cornerstone,
tried stone of witness—the rock of my salvation,
hewn from the Savior, *"more than friend or life to me."*

I bring a stone engraved with her name, Brenda Joyce,
my love, the wife of my youth in whom I rejoice;
white topaz, the symbol of my pure love for you.

A stone engraved with another name "*Melissa,*
Melissa, Belissima", a new day dawning;
my firstborn joy, my sweet, a birthday gift for me.

Psalms of Remembrance

A lively stone with another name, Angela,
"*Si, Mi Angelita es muy bonita.*"
burst forth on the scene the day before Pentecost.

Stone upon stone—*El-Beth-el*—I build this altar.

A stone with jagged edges I hold in my hand:
disappointments and stillborn dreams lie at my feet,
wet with red, splattered with blood of miscarried sons.

I bring a piece of onyx, black stone of mourning,
wrenched from the valley of the shadow of death,
this dark marker of man's appointment once to die.

I rise to find a precious stone, a star sapphire,
symbol of healing and wholeness for my family,
to remind me of *Jehovah Rapha's* promise.

Cameos carved with the touch of the Master's hand,
Jasper-clear, on backgrounds of God's abundant grace,
Reflect countless blessings and promises to come.

Stone upon stone I build this altar—*El-Beth-el.*

Gathered from quarries of African origins,
gemstones for my parents and unknown ancestors,
all those who "sang a race from wood and stone to Christ."

I offer a ruby, priceless gem of passion,
my zest for life, blessed to explore varied careers—
wordsmith and pharmacist and teacher of God's Word.

Stone Upon Stone

Another precious stone—amethyst remembrance—
whispered words, beckoning to a higher calling,
a whetstone to sharpen the tool to pierce my ear.

Final stone of hope, capstone to complete my life,
standing on tip-toe, awaiting the golden note,
blessed hope of Christ's appearing in my lifetime.

El—stone upon stone—*Bethel*—I build this altar.

In the center of this altar burns fire, white-hot
as the cloven tongues appearing at Pentecost,
a flaming fire, refueled by the oil of blessing,
this unction, anointing, ignited by the spark,
tabernacled in me twenty-six years ago;
consuming desire, empowered by the spirit,
seeking to forge with words, this joy unspeakable.
Enflamed with a new name and transformed to offer
all I am and all I ever hope to become,
a living sacrifice, wholly acceptable,
a lively stone, known, read by all with eyes to see.
So I return to teach the meaning of these stones.

El—stone upon stone I build this altar—*Beth-el*

> San Antonio, TX
> June 17, 1993

Psalms of Remembrance

A Song of Celebration

*Commemorating the Sixth Anniversary
of
Ambassadors for Christ Fellowship
Columbus, Ohio
May 7, 1995*

*And God saw every thing that he had made,
and, indeed, it was very good.
So the evening and the morning were the sixth day.*

Genesis 1:31

... And the evening and the morning were the sixth day.

> From the beginning, the essence of God's "is-ness"
> flowed freely from the pure heart of very goodness,
> as He fashioned all life in His own divine way,
> formed, made, and created in glorious array,
> thus revealing the Father's good pleasure to bless.

... And the evening and the morning were the sixth day.

> As Ambassadors for Christ we work, watch and pray,
> complete in Him, the maker of our righteousness.
> We labor to enter that rest of blessedness,
> pressing toward the mark of a new and living way.

... And the evening and the morning were the sixth day.

The Song of Pentecost

Acts 2:1–4

Those with ears to hear seek your song of grace.
With no song to soothe the soul, all is lost.
Your melody makes life a quiet place
When the heart sings the song of Pentecost.

There in Eden's garden fell the first frost
Where stillborn silence chilled the human race.
The purest harmony with God was lost.
Those with ears to hear seek your song of grace.

Voices of patriarchs could not replace
The inner melody from God. At most
Their sound was an echo, only a trace.
With no song to soothe the soul, all is lost.

With the sign of blood upon the doorpost
Moses led Israel toward the promised place.
The lyrics of the Law were their guidepost.
Your melody makes life a quiet place.

Man hears life's sublime music in the grace
By Jesus Christ, who died and rose to post
A higher law that death cannot erase
When the heart sings the song of Pentecost.

Sound of rushing mighty wind: the signpost,
The prelude to the promised song of grace.
With the outpouring of the Holy Ghost,
The song of Pentecost can now embrace
Those with ears to hear.

Psalms of Remembrance

Sunday Morning Glories

*I was glad when they said unto me,
Let us go into the house of the Lord.*

                              Psalm 122:1

Tender memories embrace and entwine
like summer ivy or morning glories
climb the walls of my mind

Nostalgic images evoked by Sundays

      benign black faces
      with gold-toothed smiles
      chalk-white uniforms and
      great, starched handkerchiefs
          with crocheted edges;
      open brown hands,
      passing funeral parlor fans—
          doorkeepers in the house of the Lord

      scarlet robes and golden collars;
      organ and piano caress;
      gospel choirs sway in procession
          Walk in the light
          Beautiful light
          Come where the dewdrops of mercy shine
              bright
          Shine all around us by day and by night
          Jesus, the light of the world

hymns, anthems, and gospel songs;
    primitive antiphons
        lined, chanted, moaned;
    lining out to raise
    a round of Dr. Watts
        A charge to keep I have
        a God to glorify
        a never-dying soul to save
        and fit it for the sky

sermonic shades of show-nuff preachin
    talkin bout Moses and Joshuway
        Say Amen somebody
    Old man Daniel and de Hebrew Boys
        Preach it, brother, preach. . .
    'Zekiel's wheel in de middle of de wheel
        Can I get a witness
    talkin bout Jonah in de belly of de
    whale
        Well. . .Well. . .

Bittersweet reflections of a way of life:

    selling dinners: chicken, chitlin, barbecue;
    budgets, benefits, and conference claims;
    song fests and love feasts;
    bake sales, bazaars, and baby contests;
    gleaners, raffles, Miss C.M.E.
    guest choirs and visiting churches
        with A and B selections
        in gospel extravaganzas
    prayer meeting, Epworth League, and
        Sunday School;

testifying services and watch meeting:
>   *talkin bout the goodness of the Savior*
>   *in these last and evil days*

sisters shoutin and gettin happy
under disquieting moves of the Spirit
that always made my "Ma-dear" cry;

communion, carnivals, and candy sales;
Men's Day, Women's Day, afternoon teas;
building funds and mortgage burning;
weddings, funerals and fashion shows;
picnics and pew rallies;
altar calls and revivals;
>   "opening the doors of the church"
>   "extending the right hand of fellowship"
>> *Just as I am without one plea...*

anniversaries and choir rehearsals;
Christmas plays, Easter speeches, Children's Day
>   pieces;

bishops, elders, local preachers;

>   standing for the doxology
>   sitting for the benediction

Mizpah
>   *The Lord watch between me and thee*
>   *whilst we're absent*
>   *one from another*

the Lord's Prayer
>   *Ouva, Father, Ouva Father,*
>   *which art in heaven*
>   *Hallowood be thy name...*

Stone Upon Stone

and Psalm 23
> *The Lord is my shepherd*
> *I shall not want. . . .*
> *Surely goodness and mercy shall follow me. . .*
> endless episodes
> unending reasons for being
>
> *. . . world without end. . .*

Amen
Amen

Taking It Personally

Isaiah 53

Cursed with a curse, He was hung on a tree.
The suffering servant bartered for a price,
Battered and bruised for my iniquity.
Behold the Lamb, unblemished sacrifice,
Offered once, Jesus Christ, my Passover.
Afflicted, stricken, smitten that God should
Freely pour out His mercy, moreover,
Lay on Him the chastisement of my peace.
From His side flowed water and sinless blood,
A new covenant established that I might cease
From dead works by a new and living way.
God's good pleasure no longer concealed
But memorialized this solemn day.
Man of sorrows, with His stripes I am healed
In spirit, mind and body, for I am
Quickened and cleansed by the blood of the Lamb.

April 15, 1998
Passover

"And David Danced before the Lord with All His Might. . . ."

II Samuel 2:14

He gently strummed the lyre to soothe the weary head
and lightly touched the strings of God's own heart.
As God's golden chosen vessel, David so yearned to be
    fulfilled,
To pour out all his oil in praise before the Lord.
He desired to deliver praise worthy of God's glory
While moving to majestic music of the inner ear.
He was anointed from above by the spirit pour upon
This shepherd-psalmist-prophet-king of uninhibited
    choreography—
Naked dancer in the foreshadow of perfect praise to
    come.

Psalms of Remembrance

David Lee, Jr. has a conversation with a tree

David Lee: Hey tree, look at me.
              You look familiar.
              Don't I know you?
              What's your name?

Tree: I'm called Tree of Heaven—
              Ailanthus Glandulosa—
              I'm a native of China,
              But I grow in this part of the world too.

David Lee: Now, I know where I know you from.
              You're the tree what use to be in the back yard.
              You're the one my mama use to make switches out of.
              Why do they call you Tree of Heaven?

Tree: I don't know. I'm sometimes called Chinese sumac,
              But most of the time they call me "Tree of Heaven."
              What do they call you?

David Lee: David Lee, Jr. I was named after my daddy.

Tree: What do you want to be when you grow up?

David Lee: Hmmm. Let me see. . . .
              I just want to be like a tree
              And be what I'm suppose to be.

                      THE END

Thanksliving

In every thing give thanks:
for this is the will of God
in Christ Jesus for you.

       I Thessalonians 5:18

What shall I render to the Lord for all
His grace? What can I say to offer praise
Worthy of His glory? How can I call
With all our being upon His name and raise
A new song from the depths of my heart?
I must do more than mouth a platitude—
To express the soul in words is an art;
Yet words cannot express my gratitude.
Mere words are empty and without merit.
"Thank you" too soon becomes a hollow phrase.
So I will worship God with my spirit
And will give thanks well for all of our days.
To live is give thanks with tongue and limb;
With each breath, each move, I *live* thanks to Him.

Psalms of Remembrance

plainsong

for Lonnie Johnson
1922-1996

Your plainsong I know by heart,
a hymn stanza learned with ease,
lined out like the flow of chanted words,
    syllables fused into a single sound:
        "*I-love-the-Lord-He-heard-my-cry*"
    raised and repeated over countless Sunday
        mornings.

Your plainsong I continue to sing, expressed not in words
but in faithful deeds borne of a heart to serve.
Your rock-solid presence like a mantle clock keeping time,
even beyond man's three score years and ten.

Your plainsong resonates and flows through my being.
I sing with strength of character, integrity,
unconsciously humming refrains, improvising
common melodies with grace notes, making my own
your plainsong that will not let go of me.

Born for Luck

*Who through faith, subdued kingdoms, worked righteousness,
obtained promises, stopped the mouths of lions*
                                        Hebrews 11:33

"Young man, you're born for luck!" the old wise woman said.
"Good things happen to you. It's written on your face."
Like seeds, her words lay dormant deep inside my head,
As she spoke of the fortuitous flow of grace.
Now I see God opens windows of time and chance.
Though some may call it merely serendipity,
This unending series of divine happenstance
Reveal God's favor in this synchronicity.
Now I understand we live by faith and obtain
Promises defined by such a synchronous flow.
Only an infinitely wise God can explain
The passion of His desire that we might know.
With enlightened understanding I now discern
That grace crescendos in the hope of Christ's return.

Your Life Is A Book

Your life is a book, and everyday is a page.
You cannot deny the pages of your own book,
because you've already written into the pages of life.
And that life will be open in the eyes of God.
When the book is finished, you cannot deny it.

                                        Elijah Pierce

Your life is a book, and everyday is a page.
We all write our lifestory, whether as fool or sage.
Printed words in boldface type impress to curse or bless,
Revealing a full measure of failure or success
In applying our hearts unto wisdom as we age.

No one knows the future nor can anyone gauge
The impact of a solitary life with its message.
Each word of our history continues to stress
Your life is a book.

Work heartily as to the Lord, no matter the wage.
Accept this, for it is futile to wrestle and rage
Against God's divine plan that we might know Him and
    express
His purpose, daily striving to write as we progress.
From infant to elder, through each unfolding stage,
Your life is a book.

The Gift

Remember your baptism and be thankful
West Ohio Conference United Methodist Church

Black clouds gather, as I ponder dark rumblings
of thunder in rapid succession, like barrels
rolling down wooden stairs. Flashes of lighnting
splinter the darkness behind tightly closed eyes.
Out of prayer and meditation flows a peace,
an ominous peace, a strained relief with a
prescient sense, forecasting an approaching storm.
In the interstice of clean scent of silence,
from this quietude a wondrous gift takes form.
With child-like naivete I would avoid the storm
For fear that rain would somehow spoil my play.

At the edge of abysmal blackness, listening
to my solemn echo and many muted
voices: A capella cantata—choral
thunder—prelude forewarning of the gift to come.

Then the fierce unbridled maelstrom, catacylsmic,
rhythmic storm, descending now without warning,
all engulfing geyser spewing bittersweet
cathartic—surging, purging, cleansing, rinsing.
Overwhelmed by the fullness of the flooding,
though drowning, I now embrace the wondrous gift.

Psalms of Remembrance

My tongue unleashed in new-found freedom of vowels
and sounds beyond my human understanding;
out my innermost being a spring erupts,
flowing crystal syllables, like a river
of living waters, coursing a path all its own.

Without warning as in the beginning, the storm,
with its mighty rushing wind, quietly abates,
suddenly subsiding, bringing now a milder
summer breeze laced with hints of lavender, lilac,
gently caressing sounds of wind chimes and celeste
and tranquil rain, freely falling latter rain,
flooding me entirely.

With no outlet but my eyes, I start to weep
at my own wretchedness, writhing in disbelief,
while rejoicing for hours as a naked child—
unnoticed, unashamed.

Reading the Word of God: A Psalm of Preparation

For Ezra had prepared his heart to seek the Law of the LORD, and to do it, and to teach statutes and ordinances in Israel.

Ezra 7:10

The first words ever spoken
flowed from the lips of God
who taught Eden's generation
to speak the holy language
in the garden watered by the river with four branches

Since God foreknew mankind
would record the spoken Word,
God gave an alphabet,
symbols of a simple culture, of an ancient tongue

> Characters of the Scriptures
> Letters of the Gospel
> Letters of the Holy Book
> Sacred script that preserved God's Word
> every jot and tittle
> hedged and compassed about,
> fenced in on every side
> by Massoritic watchmen,
> inscribed by *Sopherim,* guarding
> and accounting for every single word
> of the sacred text
> passed on to countless generations
> for man to read in the language of the Prophets
> > in the language of our Lord,
> > in the language of the Apostles,
> > in the language of the men of God
> > inspired by the Spirit to write the God-
> > breathed Word.

Psalms of Remembrance

As I read the Holy Scriptures and seek to show
myself approved, as pupil and willing workman,
cutting straight my understanding, by not handling
the Word of Truth deceitfully but hiding it
in the innermost recesses of my spirit,
I pray: *God enlighten my mind to comprehend,*
then inscribe Your law on the parchment of my heart
and magnify these words upon scrolls of my soul,
and will You tutor me, precept upon precept,
line by line and make plain my reason for being.

With shoes removed and my hands raised in
      submission,
having entered in by a new and living way,
in this most holy place of my tabernacle,
here I long to abide, to live, to learn to serve.
As Ezra placed his ears near to the lips of God
so I fix my heart to seek God's Law and do it
and set my eyes to see clearly His Word and will
revealed that I might teach it to willing students.

Try Me

Search me, O God, and know my heart:
try me, and know my anxieties;
And see if there is any wicked way in me,
and lead me in the way everlasting.

Psalm 139:23–24

Lord, Prepare me to be a sanctuary. . .
pure and holy, tried and true. . .

Purify my motive; assay my devotion;
weigh each desire, carat by carat, dram by dram.
In the refining fire of your furnace try me.
Test the mettle of my soul; scrape away all dross,
all debris that would adulterate my intents
and leave behind the purity of ore that I
may see my face reflected in the pool of gold.
I long to take the treasure of your precious Word,
securely hide it in the lock box of my heart
and as a faithful son, hand you the only key.

Psalms of Remembrance

After the Art of the Apothecary

*And thou shalt make it an oil of holy ointment,
an ointment compound after the art of the apothecary:
it shall be an holy anointing oil.*

Exodus 30:25 (KJV)

I desire to follow recipes and not to vary
From the prescribed formulas for the remedies I need,
To compound after the art of the apothecary.

I long to work circumspectly and always be wary,
To measure and mix precisely for love and not for greed.
I desire to follow recipes and not to vary.

I recall yearning to learn from childhood days in Gary,
To weigh my decisions and follow as the Lord would lead,
To compound after the art of the apothecary.

I seek to formulate my ideal art and to marry
Vocation and avocation as one of love and need.
I desire to follow recipes and not to vary.

I attempt to move with wisdom but never to tarry
To master each prescription, to excel and to succeed,
To compound after the art of the apothecary.

The sweet smelling savor I desire my life to carry
Is the pure, holy anointing oil tempered of my need.
I desire to follow recipes and not to vary,
To compound after the art of the apothecary.

Song of Triumph

And having disarmed principalities and powers,
He made a public spectacle of them openly,
triumphing over them in it.
                        Colossians 2:15

Death, I will not succumb to your dull drum,
Nor march in cadence to your muffled dirge.
Though toward a common end all flesh must merge,
Your lifelong lament I refuse to hum.

Though I endeavor to compute the sum
Of all my days that toward this end converge,
Death, I will not succumb to your dull drum,
Nor march in cadence to your muffled dirge.

My pace in double time defies the plumb
Line dropped before life's final tide shall surge.
I have hope even death can never purge.
Though my heart may be pierced, my brain go numb,
Death, I will not succumb to your dull drum,
Nor march in cadence to your muffled dirge.

Enoch's Song

*By faith Enoch was taken away so that he should not see death;
"and was not found, because God had taken him",
for before he was taken he had this testimony,
that he pleased God.*

Hebrews 11:5

My heart's song is to so sing like Enoch,
With all that lies within me, with each breath,
That I too may walk with God and please Him,
That one day when they seek me, I shall not
Be found, for I will have been gathered, caught
Up to meet the Lord in the clouds forever,
Never to taste the bitter root of death
But savor the sweetness of His favor.
That to do His will was my sole desire—
May I leave behind this testimony
Written on the pages of pure a heart
Prepared for the marriage ceremony,
Blameless in His presence with nothing to hide,
So transformed and fashioned to be the bride.

Firstfruits

*Of His own will He brought us forth by the word
of truth, that we should be a kind of firstfruits
of his creatures.*

James 1:18

Transform and then so fashion my visage
To be like Christ, the brightness of your glory.
In your refiner's fire melt and mold me,
Cast my being in His express image:
As boldface type printed upon the page,
As a new coin minted in your treasure,
Stamped with the essence of your character
To convey the power of your message.
So saturate my spirit, heart, soul and mind,
Every fiber of my being, each pore;
So permeate my presence that I might find
My true calling as Christ's ambassador.
More than vessel, vehicle, or instrument,
Like Christ, I am firstfruits of God's intent.

Psalms of Remembrance

"If the Lord tarries..."

James 4:13–15

"If the Lord tarries" and "If the Lord will":
May these phrases ever be my preface.
With each decision may I learn to be still
And never presume to know your desire.
Though I may read your Word and apply
It diligently to my heart to do
All you ask of me, some secrets are not
Mine to know. Once more you tell me to watch,
To prepare my heart and to look above.
Whether I understand or misconstrue,
I cannot deny I have tasted your love.
God is faithful and His word is true.
In my heart the hope continues to burn
As I yearn even more for Christ's return.

Stone Upon Stone

A Psalm of Endless Praise
Psalm 150

Waters of life descend and rise again.
Rain falls and melts the mountain ice and snow.
A stream will mount and gather force to rush
Past boulders, trees, and any barricade
To end its journey at a distant shore
Where waves resound and sing in endless praise.

If waters should suppress their songs of praise,
Then sculptured faces in the earth's terrain
That span from crested peak to canyon floor
Would vocalize a melody to show
That earth was so designed and so arrayed
That every crevice in the land hums praise.

And if the rocks could not proclaim their praise,
All planted life from redwood to sage brush—
Fern and rose, moss that grows on oak—was made
To green the earth, absorb the gentle rain
To bless and serve mankind that he might know
That all the earth abounds and blooms in praise.

But if the garden lacked for all its praise,
Then lark and lamb would still reveal much more.
The lion's roar, the song of spotted thrush
Are parts of Nature's lofty hymns that flow
With every breath all birds and beasts sustain
To harmonize life's symphony of praise.

Psalms of Remembrance

Should the breath of beasts fail to utter praise,
Behold the matchless mind of man, displayed
In treasures from his hands and then explore
His graceful limbs, his tongue which speaks, to gain
A glimpse of love intended to bestow
On man alone the power of perfect praise.

But should man's tongue not flow with perfect praise,
Galaxies of countless stars would echo
Love songs from heaven's vaulted dome, relayed
To earth throughout the universe before
Celestial force or spirit power could hush
The chorus of creation's endless praise.

Waters flow with song, highlands hum their score,
While bush and bird join man in serenade
As stars sustain a psalm of endless praise.

About the Author

Described as a "real Renaissance Man," Lonnell E. Johnson represents a unique collage of experiences as a poet and speaker. He has worked as a pharmacist, information analyst, editor, administrator and director of public relations, as well as university professor. His use of original poetry, his vivid illustrations, and delightful humor also provide a special flavor as motivational and inspirational speaker.

Born in Gary, Indiana in 1942, Johnson earned his B.S. degree in pharmacy in 1965 from Purdue University and has worked as a registered pharmacist in Indiana and North Carolina. Drafted into the U.S. Army in 1967, Johnson served as a pharmacy instructor at the Medical Field Service School, Ft. Sam Houston, Texas, where he discovered the joys of classroom teaching, a passion that continues to burn. In 1978 he received his M.A. degree in English from Emporia State University and in 1986 earned his Ph.D. in English from Indiana University, where he was a Consortium on Institutional Cooperation (CIC) Fellow.

From 1985–94, he taught at Fayetteville State University, an historical Black institution in North Carolina. While at Fayetteville State, Johnson distinguished himself as teacher, scholar, and published poet. Receiving the first Teacher of the Year Award in 1989, he was also one of the co-directors of the 1988 National Endowment for the Humanities Grant—"Fiction, Social Change, and Charles W. Chesnutt's Fayetteville."

In addition he was a working board member of the North Carolina Writers' Network, serving as Vice President from 1991–92. During this time, he participated in several programs, such as Black Writers Identification Project, Young Black Writers, and Glaxo Technical Writing Project, among others.

He has written numerous biblical research articles and is author of *Ears Near to the Lips of God*, collection of poetry published in 1984. His second collection, *Sacred Jazz: Music, Mood, and Mind*, runner-up for the 1994 Persephone Press Book Award, was republished in 1998. His poem, "No Mo Blues" appears in *Literature: Reading Fiction, Poetry, Drama and the Essay,* 5th edition (McGraw-Hill). Johnson has captivated audiences across the country with his lively poetry performances with musical accompaniment.

In addition, Professor Johnson has also published scholarly articles in *The Journal of Black Sacred Music, College Language Association Journal, Minority Voices, The Mount Olive Review, The Oxford Companion to African American Literature, African American Authors, 1745–1945, A Bio-Bibliographical Sourcebook, The Zora Neale Hurston Forum,* and other publications.

Ordained to the Christian Ministry 1974, Johnson presently serves as Associate Pastor and Coordinator of Missions at Ambassadors for Christ Fellowship, a multicultural, interdenominational congregation in Columbus, Ohio.

Johnson is married to the former Brenda Warren, and they are parents of two daughters: Melissa and Angela.

About the Author

Currently on leave of absence from his position as Professor of English at Otterbein College, Dr. Johnson has established Ambassador Press, publishers of his personal testimony *Watch, Fight and Pray: My Three-fold Strategy to Combat Prostate Cancer* and this collection, *Stone Upon Stone: Psalms of Remembrance.*

www.ingramcontent.com/pod-product-compliance
Lightning Source LLC
Chambersburg PA
CBHW031256290426
44109CB00012B/599